A Healing Hug for Alzheimer's Caregivers: All About Caring, Grieving and Making Life Better

A Healing Hug for Alzheimer's Caregivers:
All About Caring, Grieving and Making Life Better

Elizabeth Postle *RN SCM1 HV FWT NVQA*

Editor and Cover Design: Lesley Postle

A GriefandSympathy.com Publication

©2013

First Printing: 2013

ISBN-13: 978-1492759805

ISBN-10: 1492759805

A GriefandSympathy.com Publication
39 Lumsdaine Street, Picton NSW 2571, Australia

www.griefandsympathy.com

email: info@griefandsympathy.com

Also available on Kindle at Amazon.com

Special discounts are available on quantity purchases by corporations, associations, educators, and others. For details, contact the publisher at the above listed address.

Contents

"We mustn't give up hope. After all, isn't that what makes us human?"

Terry Pratchett, Author and Alzheimer's Campaigner

INTRODUCTION

Alzheimer's disease is the most common form of dementia. It affects mainly the elderly over the age of 65, and by the time the age of 85 is reached, Alzheimer's affects nearly 50% of the population. Early onset Alzheimer's can also affect people below the age of 40. Worldwide there are approximately 35 million people with of dementia, with 4.6 million new cases each year. 60% of cases are in under developed countries. In the USA, there are about 5 million people of all ages with Alzheimer's and around 200,000 people with early onset Alzheimer's. In the UK dementia affects over 800,000 people. Slightly more women than men are affected, but that may be because women tend to live longer than men. The causes are not well understood and currently there is no cure. As more and more people are affected by this disease, this book aims to help those trying to cope with the day to day realities of a family member who has been diagnosed.

About the author

Elizabeth Postle began a 45 year career in nursing and healthcare in 1955 when she enrolled in a unique nursing cadet traineeship offered by the Southend Area Health Authority. Leaving her home at 16 years old she travelled by bus from the North of England to live and train in Southend on Sea.

Her long and varied career as a Nurse, Midwife and later Health Visitor and Field Work Teacher for the Hertfordshire Area Health Authority included training and working within the areas of Psychology, Sociology, Paediatrics, Child Development, Counselling, Aged Care and Dementia.

Together with her late husband Colin Postle, a pharmaceutical chemist, she continued her commitment to her nursing career as owner and manager of a high dependency, private nursing home in Norfolk, England. Elizabeth and Colin created a homely and welcoming environment in a historic old rectory for their nineteen residents, who included many with dementia. There were tears when, after fifteen years of running the home, Elizabeth and Colin retired, as they had created such a supportive and comforting haven for residents, families, and staff.

Passing on a great wealth of knowledge, Elizabeth continues to support and assist families coping with the effects of dementia, aged care and in particular Alzheimer's with this book and with her publication of www.griefandsympathy.com, a website she established in 2012.

One of the aspects of grief which interests her particularly, is the grief which is felt by those who are losing someone gradually to Alzheimer's. This grief is often overlooked by everyone as the focus is on the person with Alzheimer's. But it is often the carers and relatives who are having a tough time, coping with the loss of their loved one during a slow and distressing decline, while dealing with the stress of caring for a loved one with the multiple problems of dementia.

About this book

The aim of this book is to help those who have a loved one with Alzheimer's in the family, but it will also be useful for those starting out on a career in the caring profession. Whether you are worrying about a person who is still living alone, caring for a spouse or parent at home, or visiting a relative in a care home, this book will guide you through all the problems which may arise, and it will help you with the grief that you will face along the way.

It will enable you to make decisions and provide the best care you can, while looking after your own needs as well. The needs of the family and the carer are of prime importance, as how can you look after someone else efficiently if you are at the end of your tether yourself?

Quality of life for both those with Alzheimer's and their carers can be enriched using the techniques and activities recommended for the home and the care setting. Difficult decisions such as accepting respite care or finding a permanent care home for your relative are worked through with common sense and a positive attitude for the welfare of all concerned.

Elizabeth believes in involving the whole family and community in caring for the elderly and she has many ideas for bringing children together with their grandparents which bring much pleasure to both young and old.

Until we can prevent Alzheimer's or find a cure, what we can do for now is understand this disease as well as we can, and provide the best care and compassion for the families it affects.

ALZHEIMER'S SYMPTOMS

What are some of the early signs of Alzheimer's disease?

Many of the following symptoms can be normal signs of old age, but they may also be early signs of dementia or other conditions. Do not panic if you notice some of these. Alzheimer's disease is very difficult to diagnose and must be done by a specialist psychiatrist. It might be nothing or they could be the signs of any of many conditions too numerous to talk about here. If you are concerned about yourself or a loved one don't be afraid to consult your doctor.

Some of the early signs and symptoms of Alzheimer's may include:

Changes in personality.

Becoming anxious or frustrated.

Becoming depressed.

Becoming sleepier or sitting about all the time.

Forgetting words and names.

Inability to shop, bringing home the wrong sorts of groceries.

No longer understanding money.

Becoming extravagant.

Not doing chores or jobs.

Repeating things. Telling the same story several times.

Losing things.

Setting off to visit someone, and ending up somewhere else.

Getting lost.

Losing track of time and days.

Forgetting appointments.

One of the earliest signs of Alzheimer's disease is the inability to cope with financial matters. People lose the ability to control money and forget to pay bills. The telephone being cut off may be the first sign of trouble. A loved one who has been frugal and careful with budgeting for most of their lives can start to behave in extravagant ways. Their finances should be monitored.

Your loved one may be taken in by salesmen at the door or on the telephone, so do be careful of this.

There is no substitute for a proper diagnosis and the advice of a doctor or psychiatrist and they are very understanding. There is lots of help and support available, so don't be afraid to ask.

For later symptoms see "THE MAJOR CHALLENGES".

Case History – Sally's Story of Early Onset Alzheimer's

Sally was only 42 when her family first started noticing Alzheimer's symptoms, although they didn't realise what they were at the time.

She lived in a small village where there was only a grocer's and a hairdresser's. She went to the hairdresser's one day and when it came to time to pay she didn't know how to count out the money. She handed over her purse to the hairdresser and asked her to take what she needed. The grocer noticed the same thing and commented about it to the hairdresser. They realised that something was obviously very wrong. Sally was only 42 years old. They decided they'd better ring her husband and let him know what was going on.

Sally had always been very house proud. Her home was immaculate and she took pride in her cooking. Her husband had already been noticing that things were getting rather strange. He had found her asleep on the sofa when he got home from work, the dinner wasn't cooked and the house started getting untidy, which she would never normally have allowed.

Her friends had also noticed that she would turn up at the house, and they'd say, "I'm not expecting you today". Then they'd realise that someone else had been waiting for her and she hadn't turned up. She'd turned up at the wrong place.

Another day, a friend met her in town for their usual weekly lunch out together and she said she'd have to go into the bank and get some money. Having come out of the bank and walked five minutes down the road, she said "I've got to go into the bank to get some money".

It was a few months before these events really began to worry Sally's husband, who took her to her local doctor. She was referred to the hospital for a brain scan, and was diagnosed with early onset Alzheimer's.

Once everyone was aware, she was cared for at home for a while. Her husband took her shopping and took control of the finances. She could still do some of her jobs, but he had to leave notes all around the house, saying things like "Lunch is in the fridge, don't forget to eat". "I shall be home at 4 pm". "Your friend June rang, she's coming over at 3 o'clock". *(A calendar is a good idea too, where every day should be crossed off so it is clear what day it is).*

He had to hide the car keys, as one day he was coming home from work and he passed her driving in the opposite direction into town. He had to turn around and follow her.

She ended up at one of the local car parks in town. He picked her up and took her home and had to collect the other car the next day.

Friends and neighbours would call in and check she was OK and take her for a walk.

Her husband was still working but after a few months he realised that he just wasn't going to be able to cope with her. He couldn't afford to give up work to look after her.

She spent the last 5 years of her life in our nursing home. Sadly her son couldn't bear to see his mother like that and didn't come, but her husband visited regularly. Sally was contented enough. She used to go over to the nearby church and help the cleaners. She might dust the same pew over and over again, but she felt part of something.

GETTING A DIAGNOSIS

Alzheimer's Disease can only be diagnosed with a series of tests which may involve blood tests, memory and thinking tests, and brain scans using CT or MRI. These tests may take some time, but are not painful. It is important to get a proper diagnosis in order to rule out any other conditions or causes of dementia. It is also important to get an early diagnosis so that treatment can begin which may slow down the progress of the disease.

There are two types of medications currently used to slow Alzheimer's progression but in some people these cause side effects. There are currently no proven ways to prevent Alzheimer's disease, although lifestyle choices such as eating a healthy diet, and exercising the body and the mind are often recommended.

How do people react to being given the diagnosis of Alzheimer's if they are in the early stages of the disease and still mentally aware?

Sometimes there is initial relief that after so many months of confusion and many tests at last there is a diagnosis. There may be shock or numbness. Many people may get on with life as if nothing has happened, and it is possible to have many months or even years of near normal life. Denial is often easier in the early stages, but it is extremely difficult if your loved one is the breadwinner and is forgetting their appointments and losing their ability to control their finances.

As reality gradually kicks in, there may be a period of grief for the health they have lost. In the case of Alzheimer's there can be months before any real changes in the condition occur. A great friend of ours, Sarah, gave a wonderful description of how she coped and travelled through all the emotions of denial, anger, anxiety and then acceptance of her diagnosis of a chronic debilitating illness. Her quote: "Everything's going to be OK but only when your definition of OK has been redefined" helps you come to terms with the disease's limitations.

www.griefandsympathy.com/copingwithchronicillness.html

Two close friends who had their diagnoses at a slightly later stage in the disease actually forgot that the diagnosis had been made very quickly. But, they then became cross with their family for preventing them from driving. They didn't realise that their abilities were diminished.

Many people continue to take a day at a time, stay positive and are determined to enjoy life whilst they can. Our own personalities determine how we react to any crisis in our lives. Some will cope better than others. A supportive, positive attitude from family and friends is essential at this difficult adjustment time.

Power of Attorney, Living Will, Guardianship

Although it is difficult to face these things, it is wise to get Power of Attorney over a close relative's affairs early. It is advisable for people to give Power of Attorney to someone they trust when they are capable of understanding what it means. It avoids difficulties later on. Your loved one may also want to consider making a living will. This lays out their wishes for how they wish to be treated at the end of life, for example, whether or not to resuscitate. This can make these decisions much easier for family members at a very emotional time, as they know what their loved one's wishes were. You might like to get advice from a solicitor or your doctor about these documents.

If you are having difficulties getting any of these documents, you can also apply to the courts for guardianship.

Another important thing to discuss may be funeral arrangements. Does the family know what the person's wishes are? And have they made a will?

Case History - Coming to terms with the fact that your partner has Alzheimer's

We were friends with a couple in the village where we had our nursing home and we often chatted briefly or waved as they walked their dog. One day I met her and asked where she was going. She told me she was walking the dog. As she only had the lead and no dog, I realised something was wrong. Her husband had been coping alone for months with her deteriorating condition, trying to hide things from friends. They had no family.

She had been honoured by the French for her work during the war with the French resistance movement. It is sad when such talented people succumb to any form of dementia. Her husband, as often happens, had been trying to convince himself that this wasn't happening.

I had a chat to him and after tests a definite diagnosis of Alzheimer's was made for his wife. He coped for a few more months with her at home. She came to us to give him respite care sometimes, for a week or often just the day to join in with the therapy sessions. This gave him time off to shop or relax.

She later became one of our long term residents and he visited every day and had lunch with her. He spent Christmas day with her too. We always had a special event on the morning with my late husband as Father Christmas giving presents, crackers and the odd glass of sherry.

Some residents then went home with family for the day. Other visitors often stayed with us for the day. Like our friend, many partners would have been alone otherwise.

We were always pleased to see her husband as a lot of the time when he wasn't there, she would call his name nonstop. Repetitive speech (Palilalia) is a common behaviour pattern in those with Alzheimer's disease.

10

Another resident would wander around the home saying "To Betty, to Betty, to the par, to the par", most of the time like a record getting stuck. She had been a golfer of course.

Coming to terms with the fact that your loved one has dementia is very difficult, and there will be times when you get very frustrated with them. You will need lots and lots of patience. Try to remember that it is the disease and not your loved one who is being difficult, confused, argumentative or just plain ridiculous. Keep your sense of humour and laugh at the crazy things which happen, and it will help you to cope.

ALZHEIMER'S STAGE BY STAGE

Early Stage

The early stage may last anything from two to four years or even longer. At this stage friends and family can hardly believe that anything is wrong. Close family however can see that decision making and general coping abilities are lost. Life may continue fairly normally, but the carer will be taking on more and more of the household management and tasks.

It is important not to delay getting a correct diagnosis in the early stages however, as there are drugs and preventative measures that can be taken to slow down the progress of the disease. (For more information about ways of protecting the brain and slowing down the progression of dementia, you might find "Alzheimer's" by Dr Sandra Cabot a useful reference).

Most will be able to wash, dress and feed themselves for many months or even years if clothes are laundered and food provided for them.

Changes may be subtle, and loss of ability may not be very noticeable. But the time taken to dress or shower may get longer. They may get less and less involved in conversations, but apart from not instigating new topics they can still answer questions, smile and seem to understand.

Middle Stage

This stage can last anything from two to ten years, and can either be a slow gradual progression, or you may find new symptoms arriving very suddenly. The middle stage of Alzheimer's disease is when some of the major symptoms and challenges start to become apparent.

Long term memory will start to be affected as well as worsening of short-term memory. They may not be able to recognise people anymore. Problems with mobility, wandering, incontinence, aggression or confusion may mean that they are unable to be left alone for even short periods and caregivers will need a lot more support and respite.

These major challenges may mean that assistance of professionals in a care home setting will be required.

Late Stage

The final stage of Alzheimer's can last from 1 – 3 years. In the last stage your loved one may not be able to communicate, they may not know who you are, and they will be unable to do anything for themselves. They will be unable to control their bowels or bladder, and they may not be able to eat. By this stage, most caregivers will be unable to cope at home, as it requires a lot of work and specialised care. If you do decide to continue at home until the end, you will need a lot of professional support. See Alzheimer's Home Care and Resources chapters for advice on where you can get help.

GRIEVING FOR A RELATIVE WITH ALZHEIMER'S OR DEMENTIA

Many people believe that grief only starts when someone dies, but this isn't true. Grief begins when you, or a loved one is diagnosed with a life threatening disease. This is particularly true when that disease is Alzheimer's or dementia, as their personality may change. They may become aggressive or withdrawn, and eventually might not even remember who you are.

Shock and denial are common in the early stages for both the person who has been diagnosed and family members. You may both feel numb and unable to believe what has happened. You may refuse to accept that the diagnosis is true, and carry on as if nothing has changed. The person with Alzheimer's often forgets that they have been diagnosed, leaving family members to carry the burden of this knowledge alone.

Anger, frustration or irritability are common reactions, or you may feel weepy or depressed. It is important to know, that what you are feeling is grief, and that you need support from friends, family and even perhaps from a counsellor or doctor, especially if you are the one dealing with the demands of being the primary caregiver.

Friends and neighbours don't realise that the family are grieving because no-one has died. You won't have the same support that most people grieving may have, so you will need to ask for help and make sure you look after yourselves. There is grief because the person you loved, the personality, has gone. Yet the person is still there.

The following pages will give you some strategies for coping with grief. Make time to look after your own health and wellbeing, and then you will be in a better position to care for your loved one. With the right support and coping strategies, it is possible to find some quality of life and be positive.

Grief and loss occur when the loved one is still alive because their personality and individuality gradually disappears. Your spouse or parent with dementia or Alzheimer's is gradually changing before your eyes and is becoming more and more dependent. You grieve for the loved one you had, whilst caring for the totally dependent person they have become. Sadly, with all the focus on the loved one with Alzheimer's, the fact that their spouse or children are suffering grief is often forgotten.

This long, slow loss of a loved one is a painful, difficult time for those coping with their home care. The husband who used to do all the DIY, gardening and deal with the household finances becomes like a child who has to be told what to wear and when to eat. The wife who used to be a great cook and homemaker becomes the child again. She has to be given food to eat, she can't shop anymore as she comes home with pounds of tomatoes and nothing else. They are still with you, they have the same smile, they may appear outwardly normal, but the ability to cope alone is gone and they become totally dependent.

The worst time is when the loved one does not recognise their children or partner any more. It is a heart breaking time. Many family members find it too difficult, too upsetting to visit when this happens. This can cause friction in families. It is a time to realise that people grieve in different ways.

If the spouse is in a care home, the daily visits combined with the emptiness of suddenly being home alone can take a toll on the one left behind. It helps to accept that, although your loved one is still there, you are nevertheless suffering a bereavement and grieving for the loss of your partner.

Children whose parents have Alzheimer's are grieving too

If one of your parents have Alzheimer's you will also be suffering grief.

You gradually lose one parent to dementia, while the other may be in a constant state of crisis, coping from day to day, and needing an enormous amount of support. Your parent may be alone, and you suddenly have to become the caregiver for your parent. Suddenly the roles are reversed and children have to support parents. This can be difficult to accept, when your parents have been the ones to care for you all your life. You have lost your support from them at the time you need it most.

Accepting that you are grieving is the first step to learning how to cope with the grief and the stress of the situation.

The emotions of grief

The emotions of grief can make us feel as if we are on a roller coaster. If we understand the mix of emotions that we may experience then it will be less frightening.

In our everyday lives our moods change, they vary from very happy to very sad. From excited to anxious and worried, from contented to bored, fed-up and depressed. Emotions happen to everyone and vary almost hourly on a daily basis to everyone, everywhere. Our emotional reactions can go from the depths of despair to the heights of happiness. The scale of changes can be extreme.

The bus is late, the car won't start, we've had a row with our partner, or we've left important business papers or homework at home. These are all natural, everyday occurrences which cause changes in our mood.

Emotions are heightened at many times of our lives. Hormonal changes during pregnancy or pre-menstrual tension. Puberty changes for teenagers. Going for an interview for a job, or going for a driving test.

Mood swings and heightened emotions are very noticeable at those times. So the emotions felt when we are in grief can be even more intense, especially if they coincide with other stressful life changes such as coping with a relative with dementia.

We also have our own personality traits coming into the equation. Some people have anxiety issues over all life's everyday problems. Others appear to take the slings and arrows of life's misfortunes very calmly.

We all know people who are cool, calm and laid back, who accept everything that life throws at them with a stoic coping mechanism. Surprisingly these people can have a severe reaction to a diagnosis of dementia in the family, as even though they are normally happy go lucky, it might be the first real test and really hit them hard. The first experience of how hard life can be is a tough lesson.

The shy, withdrawn personality may want to hide away and isolate themselves. Family and friends must be aware of this and try to involve them and draw them out. They need to be watched carefully.

Others panic and worry their way through life. The reaction of a worrier to the diagnosis of a life-threatening disease can be extreme. Some people are so bereft that the only relief they get from the shock and pain is sleep. No way can they cope with the day to day stress of caring. Medical help may be needed and a lot of support.

Accept the emotions of grief for what they are - just feelings....

Tears are never far away. Accept all these feelings for the emotions and adrenaline rushes that they are. Try to keep calm. Take a few deep breaths and rationalise what is going on. Take time for yourself to calm down, or cry on a friend's shoulder when the going gets a bit tough.

We all have different approaches to life, therefore accept your own limitations, grieve in your own way and accept help when you need it.

Enduring life's difficulties, getting through it, ultimately makes us stronger. Focus on getting through a day at a time.

If you find that the lows are so pre-dominant that you feel depressed or suicidal then get urgent help from your doctor.

How to deal with grief

When feelings are high, have a weep, take some deep breaths and move on. Ring a friend, smile, go shopping, cook a meal. Carry on with your normal activities. Anything to take your mind off these negative feelings. You will learn to cope with your emotions and the severity of these feelings will ease. A huge effort has to be made to think positively and focus the mind. Keeping busy won't be difficult when you have so much to do caring for your loved one, but make time for yourself. Get a friend or neighbour in and take some time to go for a walk, or visit a friend.

Endure and survive. Bring happiness back into your own life.

When anxiety, panic and butterflies in the stomach overwhelm you, just let it wash over you like a wave. Understand that it will pass and you can learn to control it. Have a cuppa. Go for a walk. Realise that they are natural symptoms. Everyone suffers them at some time in their lives. They are not unusual.

Keep up with your friends. If you feel that some friends have deserted you, get in touch with them again. Some people are simply afraid of psychiatric illness and don't know what to say or do. So they stay away.

Organise, organise, organise

When the going gets tough, the tough get going....

It would be so easy to sit in the corner and wallow in self-pity, but this is your loved one. Get on with it. Do it for them. Putting your mind to practicalities is good therapy for you and helps you get through the first difficult days. Talk over what's going to happen to your loved one with other family members. Ask for the help you are going to need.

Get a routine going, and organise a regular time for you to escape and have some time to yourself. Organise meals on wheels, and a family member or caregiver to come in and help. Make a weekly timetable including free time for you and stick to it.

You may suffer a lack of confidence or an attack of anxiety even if you were previously a very confident organised person. Take each day at a time, organise your affairs slowly and your confidence will return. Learn to laugh at being a wimp! Accept that you are not super-human. You are allowed to grieve and be upset, but do try to think positive and remember all the good times. You will still find some joy in moments with your partner or parent. It will be different, but you will still have special times. It would be easy to sit in the corner and hide away. It helps no-one, least of all you.

Sleep, Laugh, Work

Try to get plenty of sleep. Try to direct your thoughts to the happy times. Have a glass of milk and a banana and drift off again. Be wary of reaching for the sleeping pills too soon. They might make you feel like a zombie and then you'll find the demands of caring even more difficult. You may be awake at night. Read, make a cuppa, write emails to friends or write in a journal or diary. You can have a nap during the day when your loved one has a sleep. Try not to worry about a change in sleep pattern and don't focus on negative thoughts when you are awake in the night.

"Laughing is our window into sanity". Stephanie Ericsson

Whatever happens to you, keep a list of things to do each day. Keep busy with family, friends, groups you belong to, or even join a new group.

Organise outings. There will be tears, but many laughs too. Laugh with friends and don't allow the self-pities in.

Keep your mind and body active. Keep ahead of household and family jobs. Take control of your finances and administration tasks. Do try to organise your own affairs as it gives you purpose and control. But if it's too hard perhaps give a family member power of attorney so they can help you.

When you let household chores and financial affairs slip behind, you can soon feel that you are not managing and inadequate feelings take over. Remain positive, be tough with yourself. Get on with things and you will find that things get easier. By keeping yourself busy you will be happier and satisfied that, yes, you can cope.

Look after your own health

As a caregiver, it's so easy to focus all the attention on the person who is ill, and none on yourself. It's important to look after your own health for both your sakes. Get plenty of fresh air and exercise and make sure you eat a nutritious diet. It's so easy to neglect your health and not bother. You will feel much better if you watch your health and it helps you to cope.

Try not to feel sorry for yourself. Seek in your local area for amenities and activities that you can join in.

Take it slowly

Don't rush any important decisions like whether or not to move house. You need to give yourself time to consider these issues. Discuss important issues with other family members and your social workers, but make your own decisions.

Keep strong

If people ask how you are, answer, "Fine", even if you are not. It's amazing how much better it makes you feel, but have one or two close friends you ring when you feel low and want a good cry.

When you need a laugh or just company go to a movie or a meal out with friends or family. Remember – you are still allowed to enjoy your life. However long or short it may be, it is precious too and shouldn't be wasted.

Living through difficult periods of life makes you into a stronger person.

UNDERSTANDING ALZHEIMER'S BEHAVIOUR PATTERNS

It may save you some emotional trauma if you can understand some of what seems to be very bizarre behaviour but which makes sense when you comprehend what is actually happening. Understanding the behaviour of those with Alzheimer's can help you develop coping strategies and activities to keep them occupied and safe.

Repetitive Behaviour

Some of the early signs of repetitive behaviour may manifest themselves as forgetfulness. Your loved one might say "I'll just get some money out of the bank". Having got the money, you walk further down the road and they say "I'll just get some money out of the bank". Alarm bells ring and you wonder what is happening. Or you might be driving along the motorway and they say "Let's stop and fill the car with fuel and get a cuppa". A few minutes after having stopped they say the same thing again. The memory pathways seem to get stuck or blocked.

Later on, this becomes much more apparent. For example, you ask the loved one to get a towel from the cupboard. Before long, all the contents of the cupboard are on the floor. If *you* get a towel, *your* brain tells you to then go and put it in the bathroom or the kitchen. With Alzheimer's the message pathways seem to get blocked so that they keep getting the towel out of the cupboard over and over again. It's like a record that gets stuck and has to be helped to move on.

If you now suggest putting a towel back in the cupboard, the cupboard will then be filled again for you. There is no point in the reaction "Why have you done that?" They will have no idea that they have done something wrong.

If you go into the kitchen and find everything out of the fridge, they might just have gone in there for some milk. Or the contents of the crockery cupboard are all out because they went for a cup. Your brain would tell you, you've got the cup, now go and get the water, or the tea. Their brain pathway gets stuck on "get a cup" so they continue to empty the cupboard.

All the contents of the wardrobe may end up on the bed when they go to get a cardigan. Or they may end up wearing several cardigans. Choosing what they are going to wear and laying it out on the bed helps with this. It seems difficult to understand until you realise that the message pathways get blocked and they continue repeating the behaviour. You can help by calmly moving onto the next task, suggesting "Let's take off a cardigan, it's hot". It can seem even more bizarre when you come in from a walk and suggest taking off a coat, and then you realise they have taken all their clothes off. You can get special garments they can wear to help prevent this.

If you understand why they are doing these behaviours, it is easier to cope. You have to be one step ahead and know how to press the stop button - by suggesting new tasks or activities. Finding jobs that are repetitive, like cleaning the brass, or sweeping the leaves can be useful. Simple tasks that they used to like doing. A daily walk can be a good idea.

Loss of financial control - telephone sales problems

Another huge concern for families is when a person with dementia answers selling calls on the phone. Families discover later that their loved one has said yes to timeshare holidays, for example, or other goods they can't afford. Of course they forget and the family have to cancel orders when the bills come in.

This brings back memories from years ago when an aunt had booked a flight for her and her husband on the first inaugural flight on Concord from London to New York, with a champagne breakfast included. Of course there was no way they could afford it. TV ads had tempted her to ring and book. The trip had to be cancelled quickly. Because the flight, and take off was all shown on TV, she was always telling people she went on it.

That too is common. A child told me recently that his Grandma keeps telling him she has been to the Olympics because she keeps seeing the ads on TV.

Only last week a friend rang to tell me about an old lady who had booked herself a holiday to Austria. She had been persuaded by a selling phone call. Of course she couldn't afford it and had no means of getting to the airport for the flight. They had to contact her son quickly for him to cancel it. He lived several hours drive away from his mum.

To avoid these problems, it is probably a good idea to put some sort of lock on the phone, or unplug it when the loved one with Alzheimer's is home on their own in the early stages

Forgetfulness regarding money and valuables

People with early dementia can't believe that they are incapable of remembering and will blame family and friends. If they buy things and forget and then realise they have less money in their purse than expected, they will think they have been robbed or will blame friends or family who have visited.

They will give away items, forget and then accuse the family of stealing.

Valuables should be itemised and preferably kept in a bank. Family members should always discuss what items they have been given.

In a residential setting no valuables should ever be left with the loved one. Any money should be left in the care of the manager. Caregivers are trained not to accept gifts, or to inform the manager and the family immediately. It is sad but loved ones do forget at this stage and accusations can be difficult.

Caring for those with Alzheimer's disease and understanding their behaviour is not easy. It all takes a lot of patience and supervision.

Coping with behavioural problems

I'm often asked how to cope with problems such as fidgeting, banging a fork against a cup, overeating or wandering. Quite often the answers to these questions are the same. Dementia is a confusing, frustrating and anxious state to live with. Those who are still aware will tell you this, - life seems to be spent in a sort of fog. The anger and despair is always taken out on the one closest to them. They lose the ability to concentrate, to read books or watch TV. This leads to boredom and they often want to just wander, fidget, or overeat, just looking for something to do.

One of the things which helps is to have a tray near where they are sitting. On it always have a beaker (with lid if needed) of water. People with Alzheimer's often don't drink enough fluid and dehydration can make anyone irritable. Being thirsty is often confused with being hungry so this, as well as boredom, can cause the overeating. They will pick up the drink many times automatically so make sure it's filled up. If hands are busy and water drunk regularly from the constant supply on the tray, the need to overeat may be forgotten. We can only hope. Keep all food out of reach as much as possible. Sweet foods in large quantities are not good for them.

What I call 'Fiddling fodder' is worth its weight in gold! On the tray also have some postcards, old birthday or Christmas cards. Some magazines with lots of pictures or an old photograph album of family (not one you would hate to get ruined). Keeping hands busy helps to dissipate the nervous energy and the boredom.

COMMUNICATION

When loved ones are getting to the stage of not responding readily to speech, making use of all five senses comes into play. People with Alzheimer's may lose the ability to understand verbal direction or communication, but often the physical senses, especially touch last longer in their lives. Part of our job as carers is making as much use of these five senses as possible.

For example, I read recently about a caregiver who found they got much better responses if they sang messages rather than spoke. If they sang "Come and get your tea" they got more response than if they spoke the message. I often used that strategy with people I cared for. Some of my carers needed confidence to put it into practice as they felt a bit silly, but everyone enjoyed it, and it got a good few smiles from other residents too. Another carer got a better response if she pointed to a seat at the table or gestured for the loved to come. Any strategy that helps can be useful.

Some communication problems may have nothing to do with the Alzheimer's but are simply the effects of old age.

Sight

Checking that the eye sight is still good is important. Make sure they have regular optician's appointments. Many carers have found that signing or gesturing bring better responses than speech with some people. Doing the actions for brushing teeth, or doing up buttons, whatever you are encouraging them to do, may be easier for them to interpret than the verbal suggestion.

When you want a loved one to go to the table to eat, often a gentle hand holding and guiding them can be sufficient. When you say "come to the table for tea", they may have forgotten what or where the table is, so a simple gesture and an arm for support may be much simpler, along with a song and a smile!

Sight can also play a calming role. Taking a walk by the water or in the park, watching the children feeding the ducks are activities which stimulate our awareness of our beautiful surroundings.

Hearing

People with dementia can get even more confused if their hearing is impaired too. A silent world can make it impossible for them to understand. Carers should always make sure that hearing aids are functioning, batteries working and get a doctor to check ears for a build-up of wax from time to time.

During the early stages talking books are very useful and can keep them happy for longer, when concentration for reading is diminishing. Music from their own era can often get a good response and sing alongs can be enjoyed even if the response is just clapping or stamping feet. Words from popular songs are often remembered. Playing their favourite music can be very calming too.

Smell

We all love the smell of baking bread or a casserole cooking and also the smell of newly mown grass. Senses can be also stimulated by picking and sharing flowers during walks. Giving the loved one flowers which are scented, like lavender, can give enjoyment. Nowadays, many warming wheat packs or pillows are combined with lavender which can encourage sleep with some individuals. If your loved one had a favourite perfume, this too may bring back memories and reach them.

Taste

Diet is important and keeping to any special needs and likes encourages a good appetite. Even when the loved one needs to be on a softer consistency diet, just liquidising the roast beef, potatoes and pumpkin for example, as you are dishing up for the rest of the family keeps the tastes of the meal intact. Some beakers have larger holes for soups etc. and many people can feed themselves longer using these. When they are fed their favourite desserts or treats this too can be calming.

Touch

Touch is a vital sense which keeps us safe. However it is a pleasurable sense too and those with dementia enjoy holding hands or going arm in arm for walks. They find comfort in having the face, hands and legs massaged with creams. This can also help muscle tone especially in someone less mobile. Stroking a beloved pet or a cuddly toy gives comfort too. Some love the satin edges around blankets or cushions. Just the feel of different textures can give interest for a while.

Supervised showers and baths also give the comfort of warm water on the skin and the stimulation of back washing.

SUPPORT FOR PEOPLE WITH ALZHEIMER'S LIVING ALONE

When a person with dementia or Alzheimer's lives alone, this can be a monumental problem for families or neighbours. It is a constant worry for families who may be coping with full time work and children and who might live a distance away. Neighbours may be the only ones really seeing what is going on, and it is a big responsibility for them.

Early signs

When families visit, the home shows signs of neglect. There are signs of personality changes. When friends or family are due to pick them up the loved one may ring several times to make sure they are coming, then forget anyway. They may shop, forget they have spent money and accuse a friend or family member of stealing.

They often start to imagine that people are trying to break into the house or items have gone missing which they had actually given away to family.

Loved ones who had downsized to a flat have been known to ring months later to say, "Someone has stolen all my furniture and left me this other cheaper stuff" - they had totally forgotten the move.

Others may wander back to the house they used to live in and complain all the locks have been changed.

They may be forgetting to shop or eat. The real fear is them becoming a danger to themselves and others. They may leave a pan on the stove and start a fire, or inadvertently leave a gas ring unlit. These are extreme of course, but monitoring deterioration is essential.

Assessment

It is important when a person with dementia lives alone that they get adequate supervision and support. The main consideration in any of the carers' discussions is whether they are safe to be left alone.

The following questions need to be answered:

Are they likely to leave a pan on the stove or an iron on?

Can they be a danger to themselves or neighbours by leaving the gas fire on unlit?

Will they wander off and get lost?

Are they likely to try and drive?

Will they keep themselves clean?

Are they capable of feeding themselves properly?

If families feel there is a marked deterioration it can be a good idea to take the loved one on the usual holiday to their home or stay with them for a few days. Being with them for more time gives a better picture of how mother, father, aunty or uncle is coping. Neighbours who have been friends for years are often able to give details of the changes they see.

Ways of supporting those living alone

Some problems can be sorted by:

having central heating systems on and set at comfortable temperatures;

leaving flasks of tea and ensuring the hot meal of the day is given when the care workers are present;

leaving sandwiches for other meals;

giving the person a tracer bracelet to wear in case they wander away.

If they are resistant to stopping driving, they can be asked to take a driving test or be assessed by their consultant. Sometimes, it takes someone in authority to tell them that they can't drive anymore. They may forget, so it is a good idea to remove car keys from the house, or even arrange to sell the car.

It can be possible to support the person living alone for a longer period of time if the right support is put in place. For example, extra home care could be arranged to wash and dress the loved one in the morning and help them to get to bed at night.

All the relevant services need to be organised. Meals will need to be delivered. Visits from carers should be arranged and neighbours alerted. If you are lucky and the person has kind and helpful neighbours, you can leave contact phone numbers with them in case of emergencies.

With early stages, however, they are puzzled. A dear friend used to say "all these people keep turning up with food and looking round my house". The person with Alzheimer's doesn't realise that anything is amiss and are not used to strangers. Some might refuse to accept help which is another worrying time for the families.

Those with Alzheimer's may cope well for years with support from meals on wheels or family and friends shopping for them. But when deterioration is becoming more obvious all agencies involved should be made aware. It is important to inform their doctor, nurses, social workers and all family members. A case conference is often organised for agencies to discuss all the concerns. Regular monitoring should be carried out by their consultant and psychiatric team.

Getting the person with Alzheimer's to accept help

Tactfully introducing help at this point can be very difficult. Patience is needed until help is accepted during these early stages. When someone with dementia is still aware of many things they may refuse the intrusion into their home. They think they are still coping as well as they used to. All offers of extra help may be refused. One friend used to say that all these strangers kept turning up with food at her door, as if she needed charity. In more lucid moments they may realise what they are there for.

One family I knew employed a housekeeper to share part of their mother's home so they could keep an eye on her. The mother thought she was a lodger and liked the thought of extra rent. I have also known a family member move in as a lodger so that they could monitor their loved one's condition.

Concerned family members may suggest a visit to the doctor but they are likely to be told by the loved one living alone that they are fine and don't need to see anyone so it can be difficult to persuade them to get help.

Some strategies might be:

If it is the flu vaccination season offer to take them to the surgery for that.

Suggest that most people over 65 have yearly blood checks just to make sure all is well and offer to take them. Suggesting a health check is easier for them to accept.

Let the doctor know what is happening. The doctor or community nurses might visit and say they are visiting all the elderly living alone.

Talk to other friends and family about your suspicions so that they can visit and assess the situation too.

Meals on wheels may be rejected but ordering from a company and the loved one choosing meals, may be more acceptable.

Would they accept help for the major cleaning jobs? Or perhaps you can get someone to supervise them by pretending they are there to clean or iron for them. This too gives an element of supervision.

Even when care or meals have been accepted they often forget and complain that all these strangers keep arriving with food or to clean the house and they think it is very rude. Don't be surprised when they won't let them into the home.

ALZHEIMER'S HOME CARE

The Alzheimer's journey is a long slow road, from the early months of investigation to diagnosis. Then there may be months of almost 'normal' behaviour when the family think there has been a mistake. This is the early stage of having to accept there is a problem. It is very difficult to face. But, it is an on-going process and you and your loved one can have many happy times during these years. During the early stages friends and family may not even realise that anything is wrong as many of the early signs of Alzheimer's disease are also typical of simple old age.

Families can cope with early Alzheimer's symptoms at home for many years with psychiatric care teams giving help and support. As long as clothes are put out and food prepared for them, many can cope with feeding and dressing themselves for a long time.

However, eventually, the caregiver will have to take on more and more responsibility. See the following list for a summary of the caregiver's role.

What being a caregiver involves

This list includes most but probably not all of the tasks that will be your responsibility if you take on the care role:

Deal with all aspects of household management, pay bills, do the grocery shopping, organise menus and do the cooking and cleaning.

Make decisions, especially about matters such as driving.

Help with all aspects of washing, toileting, dressing, feeding and activities. This will differ from person to person and will increase as time goes on.

Be the gardener and chauffeur.

34

Do the laundry and ironing.

Handle all financial affairs. Get power of Attorney from your solicitor. (Also, has your loved one made a living will? Have that available in case of urgent hospital admissions.)

Organise all medical or other appointments and make sure your loved one can get to them.

Organise and administer all pharmacy medications.

Be the nurse for dressings or other simple first aid needs.

Be the safety officer for the home, check for any hazards that could result in falls or burns.

Organise visits to family and friends or other social outings.

Set up days out for them at Alzheimer's groups.

Organise respite care as you will need the break. Don't feel guilty because you need to keep well.

Don't be afraid to ask for as much help as you can get from family, friends and support services (see below). You will find that 24 hours in a day is not enough.

When you make the decision to become a carer you need to be aware just how time consuming it can be. To get a loved one up, showered, dressed and to breakfast can be around an hour and a half. You cannot rush them. Then you have to clean the bathroom, make the bed and clear up after breakfast.

After that you may be going to appointments, for a walk or getting lunch ready.

There is all the laundry to organize too. Spilled drinks and food create more laundry and it is a huge task keeping up with it all. Extra laundry, especially in winter can be a huge strain on elderly carers. (Your loved one may be able to help hang the washing or fold dry laundry. Let them help as much as possible.)

Being a carer involves a lot of skills. Whether or not you can cope will depend on your health, age, the suitability of the home environment and how much support is available. If you are the household bread winner as well, this may prove too much. Do not feel guilty if you cannot cope. Not everyone can.

Alzheimer's home care support services

Make use of the services available to you. Services can vary from country to country so do check your local area. The most commonly available include:

Doctors will refer to specialists and give prescriptions for all medication required. They can also provide information about all the other services available in your local area. You should be provided with a telephone number you can use for emergencies or if you cannot cope any longer. Don't be afraid to ask for any support you need.

Social workers may visit to assess the level of care needed and provide a letter which says that high dependency care is required. The carer can then apply to homes for respite care.

Psychiatric nurses or social workers support the caregiver during any crisis. They also do home assessment visits to make sure that the home is suitable and carer is capable of providing the care needed.

District nurses may be asked to visit, to give insulin or provide other nursing procedures.

Caregivers can visit to help shower, dress and get the loved one up in the mornings. This gives the full time carer a chance to shop or do home jobs.

Occupational Therapists may visit the home and assess for any extra aids needed.

Meals on Wheels may be available.

Dietitians could be needed to advise on aspects of special dietary requirements.

Incontinence advisors can provide advice on all aids available.

Health Visitors can give advice on all agencies available and any health issues that you may have.

Pharmacies keep individuals medicine records on computer and will often home deliver prescriptions. They can also provide daily doses in special dated and timed containers, easy for carers or those living alone. This also provides a safety net as they can check on what medications are being taken. They can also give advice when needed, on many health issues.

(An elderly friend went on holiday and left her ready packed medications in the kitchen. She rang us in a panic. All we had to do was ask her to get the phone number of the nearest pharmacy to her hotel which she did. We then rang her local pharmacist who was able to email the prescriptions to the pharmacy near the hotel. They delivered them to her within an hour. It is always worthwhile to know your local pharmacist and keep your information on their records.)

Alzheimer's groups are a good source of information and a place to meet other carers and share common difficulties.

Forums on the internet share and solve many common issues. (See our Resources chapter for website addresses).

Day respite care is available in most towns. They can go for one or two days in the week, usually from 10am to 3pm, have lunch, play bowls or bingo and often go out on day trips. Transport is provided if wanted. The carers can use the time to have a cup of tea and chat with other carers or go out to meet friends. Having some time to themselves is vital.

Respite holiday care can be available. Do visit homes in the area early in your caring days to establish what is available. Talk to homes' managers to find out costs and what state sponsorships there are. Book early, as they do get full quickly.

Caregivers' benefits. There is a small monetary payment for caring full-time at home in some countries, and some also offer financial help with holiday respite days, so find out what is available in your area.

Rehabilitation Centres. The local hospital may have a rehabilitation centre attached. If your loved one has an accident or an injury they may be admitted. Then full assessments can be done. Physiotherapy sessions or massage may be provided to help mobility. In the early stages pool therapy can be beneficial, but never leave a person with dementia near a pool or bath alone.

No carer should ever feel that they are coping alone. There is help out there. If you have been inadvertently overlooked ask your doctor for the information.

Alzheimer's home care needs a lot of organisation

Routines get established at home, a day care facility booked for one or more days a week. Day carers may be booked to give opportunities for the carer to go shopping or to dental appointments. There is a lot to organise, and it is important to take care of yourself as well as your partner. Talk to family and friends about your concerns, and arrange the help you need. You may need help to organise your finances or housing arrangements.

Don't try to do it all yourself. You need respite, time for yourself.

It may be possible to take your loved one to friends' homes for lunch or to the movies, just as you could take along a child. I know some people who have taken their loved one on holiday to a hotel and coped well.

You'll need to make a decision about the loved one driving at an early stage. You might have to sell their car, saying money is tight, or just hide the car keys. If you can get the doctor to write down that they are not allowed to drive, that might help you to convince them, as they often forget that they can't drive anymore.

Coping with Specific Tasks

In the bathroom

At first, you might just need to put toothpaste on their toothbrush, and put out a cloth and a towel and a comb. It's good to encourage them to keep doing these things as long as possible. Gradually more and more supervision may be needed until eventually, you might need to bathe them yourself.

Some develop a dislike of the bath or shower. If this is the case, try and organise their wash for a time when they are normally calm.

Get everything you need together first, and make sure the room is warm. Check the water temperature is comfortable. You should already have got temperature controls on all your taps to make sure they can't scald themselves.

You might find that a sponge bath is more acceptable and easier some days.

Toileting

Your loved one may forget where the bathroom is, or know something is wrong, that they need to go, but don't know what to do about it. It's a good idea to take them to the toilet every hour or two whether they say they need to go or not to avoid accidents. And look out for signs such as agitation, pulling at clothes which may mean they need to go. See also the section on incontinence below.

Dressing

The carer may find that the loved one puts on odd shoes or mismatching outfits and does not appear as the smart person they used to be. Reminding them to clean their teeth or comb their hair may be all that is needed.

They may get an obsession about a favourite dress or shirt to wear. Getting it washed and dry while they are asleep may be the way to keep the calm, or you could buy another and have two or three the same.

Your loved one may start to get confused when dressing themselves and you may find that clothes have been put on the wrong way which is particularly difficult for men when trousers end up back to front. They may put things on in the wrong order, or put on two or three cardigans. Putting out the clothes in the morning, in the order they need to be put on can help with this.

It will become clear to you when it is time for you give more help but always let them do as much as they can.

If your loved one has a habit of undressing at inappropriate times, you can get special outfits online which they find more difficult to remove.

Feeding

Most people with dementia will be able to feed themselves during the early stages. As time goes on they may need more help, perhaps by cutting up their food for them. Later on, you may find they need to have mostly finger food, or liquids in feeder cups with lids as they find it more difficult.

Appetite can vary enormously. Some like to eat all the time, while others may not want to eat at all. To encourage the appetite, offer small snacks regularly, or perhaps give smoothies or warm malted drinks.

If chewing seems to be a problem, get their mouth checked by a dentist and make sure their dentures fit well if they have them. If they start to have difficulty with swallowing, you can liquidise meals in the blender so they can be fed more easily.

Always make sure they have a cup of water with a lid next to them so that they don't get de-hydrated.

Caring for someone at home is a 24 hour a day, 7 days a week commitment. They need constant supervision and help as a child would. It can be hugely satisfying but it is very frustrating at times and each day brings new challenges. Sometimes you feel that you are doing all this work for little thanks, as your loved one is in a world of their own.

We do it because we love them, but do realize your limitations. Share the care with other family members where you can and get as much respite as you can.

41

You do a wonderful and very difficult job and deserve a medal. If it all becomes too much, you did your best, that is all any of us can do.

Coping with specific problems at home

Mobility

Wandering may be coped with initially using tracer bracelets or extra locks on garden gates or doors. A small bell attached to doors inside may be useful to alert you to where your loved one is going. If you have the opposite problem and your loved one has difficulty walking, you may find a walker, higher chairs and other simple disability aids are enough to start with.

Handrails may be required to help with getting up steps to the house or in the bathroom. Shower stools may be needed. Non-slip mats are essential for safety. Where possible waterproof sanitary chairs can be pushed into the shower room so that the person is seated whilst showering. Most over 55s new build complexes these days have doors wide enough for wheelchair access and also large shower rooms. Sadly most of us have to compromise and deal with what we have.

Lounge chairs that lift people out for ease of sitting or standing up are available. Occupational therapists can assess your home and recommend aids such as a chair lift in the home when climbing stairs is a problem. Walking aids or wheelchairs may be required. Many of the aids may be supplied by local authorities when you are providing full time care or if the person is living alone.

Sometimes a room in the home can become the care room if immobility becomes a problem. Even special style hospital beds can be provided, with the monkey pole to help with sitting and cot sides to prevent falls. Commode chairs and urinals can also be supplied. Do check what is available and what would be best for your loved ones needs.

42

Crawling

There are some who only want to crawl. You stand them upright with help, but all they want to do is go back to crawling around. They appear to be happy doing this. It is the carers who get upset. If the surroundings are carpeted and the loved one isn't coming to any harm then wrap the knees to stop any chaffing and see what develops. Perhaps consult your specialist for advice. The brain isn't fully understood and it is probably due to a particular part of the loved ones brain being affected by the illness.

Aggression

One of the worst problems for the caring family is when their beloved parent or partner becomes aggressive. If you think of the tantrums of the toddler who has difficulties with controlling their volatile emotions, the same thing is happening here. However with a large adult male or physically fit adult lady aggressive behaviour can be very difficult to control and frightening for the caregiver. They then need more expert help from psychiatric teams and emergency calls are often needed. Don't feel a failure or guilty. These are patterns of behaviour common with some people with Alzheimer's disease.

Aggression can sometimes be managed by taking their mind off what is upsetting them. Always agree with them where possible and try to distract them.

Sometimes the problem can be a simple one that they want to go to the toilet and can't think what to do. That is something else that the carer has to remind them to do. They have very similar behaviour patterns to a toddler in some respects.

Incontinence

Taking them to the toilet regularly and reminding them to go can prevent many accidents. Very early in the home care situation a waterproof mattress cover should be put on the bed. Incontinence pants may be very useful but leaks do occur. At first it is possible to cope with incontinence pads in various sizes either washable or disposable. They can be used on chairs as well as on the bed. You can buy incontinence aids at shops for disability aids or online.

In summer when it is hot leave all the top bedding off. They may go to sleep on top of the bed and accidents can soak everything. The special pants do not always soak up all the volume of urine.

When the person is still aware it is difficult for them to accept incontinence aids but even younger, fit people can have problems. There are incontinence advisors who can show all that is suitable for individuals. Incontinence can be the reason for the prevention of visits to friends and family.

Safety

This is a big issue and you will need to make sure that your home is safe for them.

Always use a fixed fire guard where there are open fires.

Use a safety guard for cooker tops which are available at mobility aid shops and online.

Always supervise or put hot irons or kettles out of reach.

Keep all hazardous materials, such as bleach, cleaners, paints etc. locked away.

Make sure hot meals or drinks are served at a safe temperature.

Keep sharp knives or scissors out of reach or in a locked drawer.

Always have slip mats in shower rooms and baths.

Install shower stools and grab rails where needed.

Have temperature controls fitted on all taps and shower heads so they can't scald themselves.

Remove locks from the inside of bathrooms, toilets and bedrooms.

Lock all windows on the first floor or above of homes.

Lock outside doors and/or keep a door chain on so they can't wander off and get lost.

Keep medications out of reach and preferably in locked cupboards.

Never restrain anyone, rather leave areas which are safe for them to wander. Make sure there are no worn carpets or rugs which they can trip over.

Keep a night light on so that they are safe if they get up in the night.

Hallucinations or delusions

Sadly, people Alzheimer's may have difficulty in telling what it real and what is not. They may imagine they see or hear things or people who are not there. They might think what they see on the television is real. There are all kinds of ways in which they may become confused. Remember that however ridiculous or strange the things they say, it is the disease talking, so try not to get frustrated with them.

It is best not to argue with them when they see something which is not there, or believe something is true or real when it isn't. It is easier to agree with them, and then try to distract them with an activity or a walk.

They may get very agitated if you try to convince them they are wrong. If the television is showing disturbing images or violence, turn it off as they may get frightened, and try and create a calm atmosphere.

Hallucinations or delusions may be symptoms of infections or fever, so take their temperature and if they have a high temperature, or their confusion is new or different, consult the doctor.

Minimising Sundown Syndrome Symptoms

Sundowning is the name given to a condition which affects some people with Alzheimer's who become more agitated and distressed in the evenings.

Whatever the cause of the agitation, caregivers can try checking several things:

Do they need the toilet? Sometimes they know something is wrong but may have forgotten what to do or where the toilet is. Having regular toileting times or reminding them to go can help.

Are they constipated? This too can cause some agitation for them.

Have they eaten much today?

Could they be thirsty? Always have mugs of water available for them to help themselves to drinks. Dehydration can cause agitation and they cannot understand why. Monitor how much fluid intake they have in a day.

Are they sleeping too long during the day time? An afternoon nap is good but not too long or the night sleep is disrupted and evening wandering becomes more likely.

Limit caffeine and sugar to the morning hours.

Are they bored? Simply wondering what to do? Try giving them a tray of activities cards to look at and old magazines. A doll to dress or a cuddly toy. See our Activities for People with Alzheimer's chapter.

Taking them for a walk sometimes calms and settles them. It's good to make sure they get plenty of day light during the day as this helps the brain to adjust to the day/night cycle. If you can keep routines of meal times, walks, activities and rest times going as long as possible this helps. Like children they like routines.

If none of these things help, it is a good idea to consult the doctor in case a change in medication or timing of medication may help. The doctor can also rule out infections, pain, or drug interactions as the cause of the distress.

Sadly, aimless wandering and other distressing behaviours can become part of dementia in the middle stages, but there are lots of little hiccoughs along the way that can be resolved if the problems are just that they cannot express their needs adequately. Carers need to be able to know what their loved one is trying to tell them, the same as a new mum with her baby gets to know the differences of meaning in each cry.

Caregivers need a medal for coping each day with the many challenges they face. Many carers feel isolated and are scared to discuss problems in case they are seen as inadequate. This is far from true. We all need to pool ideas on care giving. Good Luck

If you reach crisis point....

Symptoms and deterioration in condition can vary from the mild and hardly noticeable to the severe over days or months. Often families are waiting for a crisis point. As each crisis hits, family, doctors, psychiatric nurses, social workers, day care centres, all can give support.

Don't be afraid to ask for help. Accept all offers, as you have to look after yourself so that you can keep well and care for your loved one. Spend time with a good friend and have a laugh. Go out and enjoy yourself to have a break.

You are doing an amazing job and need all the help you can get. Many people can't manage home care as you are doing. Do realise that the time will come when it is too much and extra care is required. Congratulate yourself for all the time you did cope.

ACTIVITIES FOR PEOPLE WITH ALZHEIMER'S

Many of these activities for people with Alzheimer's are suitable for people still living at home as well as for those in residential care. People with Alzheimer's or dementia can often take part in many activities with others, but may need more supervision. Choose some suitable pastimes from the following if you are a caregiver at home, or perhaps you work at a residential facility and are looking for ideas.

The story of a good friend of mine who had from early onset Alzheimer's shows how she was able to join in many activities:

When her husband could no longer cope at home, my friend became one of our long term residents. In her late 40s she was physically fit and always dressed smartly. When our staff had first aid or fire safety lectures she always sat in and looked interested. Many of the lecturers did not realise that she was a resident.

Whenever any of the staff had tea breaks she loved to go and sit with them. A friend from the village would collect her whenever she was going for a walk or would take her into the church to help with the cleaning. She may have dusted the same pew many times but she looked happy helping. Although at this stage her ability to care for herself was minimal, she still had quality of life. Some friends from her village would come and take her for walks along the beach occasionally. Her husband took her out to the beach for long walks most weeks during his visits when it was fine.

Everyday household activities for those with Alzheimer's

Washing and dressing can take longer, often putting items out for them helps but do let them continue with these tasks as long as possible.

49

A walk every day is excellent, often they can go round a familiar route on their own or with the dog if they have been used to that. Always remember to put on hats and sunscreen.

Helping in the garden, clearing leaves or bark from the trees, collecting wood and kindling, repetitive types of jobs that they may have got used to doing.

Clearing and re-laying the open fire. Some jobs they have done for years become instinctive. They may be slow but let them do it.

Laying the table for meals, folding serviettes, helping prepare vegetables, shelling peas etc., day to day tasks which help them to feel useful.

Cleaning brass or doing some dusting is also a job they can do. They may dust the same thing several times but it doesn't matter.

Folding laundry is another activity which can help people feel needed.

Entertaining activities for people with Alzheimer's and their caregivers

Do continue to go out and visit friends for lunch or invite them to you. Don't refuse any invitations, but tell friends that your loved one might repeat themselves or there might be a little bit of unusual behaviour. You may find some friends stop inviting you. They are frightened and don't know how to react. Try not to blame them. Perhaps get in touch with them when you have some respite time alone.

Movies - continue to see any films that you know your loved one would have chosen. It doesn't matter if they fall asleep half way through.

Car rides to local parks or beaches followed by a walk are good for caregiver too.

Radio and TV can be useful, but because the concentration span is short they are likely to fall asleep easily. Too much sleep during the day can cause sleepless nights.

Audio books from the library are useful and concentration spans on them might be longer when they are listening to someone else.

In the early stages, crossword puzzles, chess or Sudoku puzzles may still be possible.

Games such as cribbage, board games, cards or jigsaws can be good and help to keep the brain active.

A sleep after lunch is good. Monitor the time of it. A good night's sleep is important.

A large tray of postcards can keep them entertained, reading and sorting them.

A fish tank is a calming, interesting thing to look at, or perhaps a bird table outside the window.

Reminiscence sessions are helpful. Old photos, pictures of early film stars, kitchen tools, old fashioned objects – these are things which can access parts of the memory and bring people alive. It is good to stimulate the brain and get people talking about old times. It gives them great pleasure.

For ladies, give her an old handbag with handkerchiefs, combs, a plastic backed mirror, a purse with the odd foreign paper money (don't want anyone to choke on coins), old keys, bobbins of cotton, plastic buckles, any item that is safe. Tidying the handbag, taking its contents out and putting them back in, is a simple but repetitive activity which can be comforting.

In my residential home, one person folded all the serviettes each day. For 20 residents having 3 meals a day it kept her busy and she felt needed. The contented look on her face was worthwhile to see.

One of the men loved to sweep leaves in the garden, another loved to move dominoes around on his tray. I imagine he was still playing with his friends in his mind.

This is the time for the carer when ask, ask, ask, for help is important. Friends and family often don't know what to do, simply taking your loved for a walk would be an enormous help. Many would be happy to do that.

Exercise

Exercise is good for you, the caregiver, as well as your loved one. It will lift your moods, and help you both to sleep at night. Even if it is just a walk around the back yard, try to get some exercise every day. Walking, dancing, or even a little stretching in the chair can be good if it is raining outside. There may be activities you can join in locally like bowling or yoga.

In 2009, I had an unfortunate accident which resulted in a broken back and both wrists. After emergency treatment I went into a rehabilitation unit for a week. It was there that I came into contact with an overseas student who was interested in doing an occupational therapy or physiotherapy degree. I don't think that the managers of this home realised just what a gem of a therapist they had in their presence. She organised an exercise class for anyone who was willing to attend which she called Fun Therapy.

She told everyone only to do what they could. At 11 am I turned up with around eight other residents all with varying degrees of disabilities, including a couple of people with dementia.

We were all sitting in a ring and she played some cheerful, rhythmic music. She started at the top of our bodies and worked down. "Everyone turn your head to the right, then to the left. Then nod your head. Then go clockwise then anti clockwise."

Next she had everyone shrug their shoulders. Shoulders circle forward, shoulders circle backwards. From the waist bend to the right, bend to the left. Kick the right leg forward, then backwards. Now the left leg forwards and backwards. Now draw a circle with the right leg first clockwise then anti clockwise. Then of course with the left leg.

There was much laughter and even singing along to the tunes she played. Arms were next, held high, down to the sides, now swimming forwards like breast stroke then backwards trying to get a big circle. Next anyone who could stood and swung their leg to the right then left. Those sitting did it from the seat. We then walked around the room, with those sitting moving their feet back and forth. Next came a marching song. We all stamped our feet and clapped and really felt that we had done a good workout.

This simple regime could be used in any care setting or in the home.

These simple exercises are fun when we laugh at our limitations, but they build confidence when we achieve small goals each day. Every day for that week we grew in numbers. We had many laughs and sing alongs yet with all our disabilities we achieved our daily exercise.

HOW TO FIND RESPITE CARE

After the diagnosis of Alzheimer's disease, a person may have months when family or friends may feel that day to day routines are as they were. They are still driving, able to be left alone or taken to stay with friends as always. They continue to be monitored by the consultant to check on deterioration.

After a while the situation may change. They may start to wander, have falls, become aggressive or become incontinent so the carer has a more demanding role, often being disturbed several times at night.

The person with Alzheimer's is being well cared for but carers can become tired, weepy and desperate for a break. It is their crisis.

Carers need to realise that it is important for them to have some respite. They will be no good to their loved ones if they wear themselves out and become ill. Feeling guilty is not productive. Many people cannot cope with caring at all, so if you have soldiered on for months or even years you should be proud of yourself, and know that you deserve and must have help now.

Don't be too proud to ask for help, take a break so that you can recharge your batteries. You are now the most important person in the family, so finding time for yourself is essential. See if you can get a short holiday, there may be respite care available in your area, or get a family member to take over the caring for a short period. If you are caring for someone at home with this illness then you are doing a wonderful job and need all the help you can get.

Day Care

There are day clubs for those with Alzheimer's and dementia in most towns and villages. Some of the activities they offer are also suitable for people in residential care.

A few hours there a week gives caregivers a rest. A change of venue for the loved one at these groups gives them a change of scene and menu. Something for them to tell you about. Do try to use gentle persuasion to get your loved one to go. It often becomes a highlight of the week.

Caregivers may be husbands, wives, sons, daughters, sisters or brothers. If there is no extended family, carers can feel isolated and lonely. The day clubs are for caregivers too. They can go and sit in another room and meet other carers, share problems over a cuppa and make new friends. Often a loved one may feel more confident at going to the day club if the carer goes too for a few visits.

The carer can also go off to shop or have a break for an hour as well. Sometimes these groups also organise outings for everyone to join in and perhaps a Christmas party for everyone too. Carers do forget that their life is important too and they need their own social life.

At first day care for a few hours or a couple of days a week may be enough. Often there is day time respite a few hours a week held in community centres or church halls. Find out what is available in your area.

Some carers say that their spouse, mother or father refuse to go. To make it easier for them, try telling them that you need to go to the dentist or doctor and that you may be a long while, so you're going to leave them with a friend who will give you lunch at the community centre. This way they often accept the group easier.

The following week you may do the same thing by saying you are going to the optician or podiatry. You may find they enjoyed their lunch out the week before and don't wish to be on their own for hours. The next week you can even say that the car needs to go in for service and that John from the group will pick you up in the coach and that you will be back when he gets home. Doing this, your loved one has a few weeks to get used to this routine, wants to go on a regular basis and also accepts getting a lift there.

Activities for People with Alzheimer's at Day Clubs

Day clubs provide activities such as sing-songs, bowls, and Bingo or group physiotherapy sessions.

Activities such as blowing up balloons for a later party in the venue can be fun.

Pets are often taken in for pet therapy, the animals always cheer everyone up and stroking a pet is very therapeutic.

One of the more recent developments is laughter therapy for people with dementia. They are entertained with magic tricks, blowing bubbles, balloon animals. Anything which can raise a giggle has to be a good thing.

Residential Respite Care

Ask your family doctor about this. A social worker may visit to assess your loved one for the care needed. It may be high dependency care. The next step is for you to visit several homes in your area and choose the one best suited to your needs. The home manager or matron can discuss financial affairs and availability of beds.

Some governments sponsor several weeks of respite care per year for full time carers of high dependency assessed clients. It is up to carers to find out what is available. Make sure you are not missing out on your benefits.

War Veterans homes give priority to ex-service personal but are happy to discuss costs and bed availability with families. In Australia, RSL clubs often provide the opportunity to discuss your needs with solicitors or experts from their care homes. Some offer appointments weekly with specialists to discuss your individual situation. Each country will have different schemes so it is important to check what you are entitled to in your area.

Once again I have heard many times that the loved one refuses to go. The correct approach is vital. Once you have found a place and a date for respite, tell your loved one that you have to go for some minor treatment and have to go away for a few days but that you have arranged a holiday for them while you are away. You can take them to see the home and the room they will have and introduce them to the staff.

Two weeks is a good time to give you space for yourself to recover from exhaustion. Your treatment may be a relaxing stay for you in a hotel, or just a break to have a rest and see friends.

Get other family and friends to visit your relative in respite while you take this time off. Usually the loved one is fine when they visit but if you visit the guilt will start again as they ask when they are going home. You can discuss how the loved one is getting on with the home's matron.

It is you coping with home care full time, so relax, rest and enjoy your break as it will pass all too quickly.

Some carers arrange with a home to have two weeks respite every three months. Others take a longer break less often.

You have to acknowledge that if you were ill your loved one would have to have long term care and these breaks are good for your health. Another important aspect to respite care is that your loved one gets used to the home and staff so that if or when long term care is needed it is not such a shock.

Whilst in the care home for respite they can have all their medical, dental, optician, and podiatry appointments, and have their hair cut. This saves the caregiver a lot of time and effort. Their medications can be assessed and any blood tests arranged. It is often a good way to get a check-up of general health issues.

Many carers are amazed at how much more alert loved ones can be when they have staff and residents around and activities going on. They also see visitors coming and going all day. At home they may sleep all day, whereas in a care setting they may be more stimulated and stay awake longer. This may help them sleep better at night. The change is often a huge benefit in many ways.

THE MAJOR CHALLENGES

When is it time to admit that you can't cope any longer with 24 hours a day caring?

Sometimes it may be an accident or illness which precipitates an admission to hospital, then a total reassessment and a forward care plan can be arranged. But often it is a build-up of problems which make caring at home too difficult to manage any longer.

These are some of the major challenges you may face when your loved one reaches the middle to late stages of Alzheimer's Disease. Not all will have all of these problems, but even one or two in combination can cause huge difficulties.

Alzheimer's and dementia affect the body as well as the mind, and it is often physical difficulties as well as behavioural changes which make it impossible to care for the loved one at home.

There are five major problems that the caregiver faces which often make them realise that they cannot cope with care at home any more. These are mobility, aggression, incontinence, safety, and sundown syndrome.

Mobility

Mobility can be a major concern. Either a loved one is too mobile- i.e. wandering, or they can go off their feet. Lack of mobility or wandering are both major reasons for needing residential care.

Wandering

At first there may be constant wandering. Some may be able to walk miles with their family having difficulty in keeping up. Physically fit people can continue to be mobile throughout the illness.

This can be a problem if the loved one gets lost. Sometimes the police have to be called to help trace someone. However GPS anklet wearing can be a solution for daytime wandering.

The worst problem for carers is when the wandering occurs at night too. The house may be locked but the carer has continual lack of sleep from being disturbed. Often the loved one's sleep pattern is changed and the difference between night and day lost. They may only sleep for a couple of hours during the day or night. It is a huge stress for carers as they need their sleep in order to cope in the day time. This is when the supervision of night staff in a residential setting may be necessary.

Caregivers should never feel guilty as no one can work seven days and seven nights a week.

Shuffling or complete lack of mobility

Others develop what is known as a shuffling gait. They slow down dramatically and this shuffling along can cause falls and injuries. The carer may find it too difficult to get the loved one up again.

The ambulance can be called to help but on a regular basis this may not be the ideal solution. These falls often lead to broken bones or other injuries needing hospital admission where future long term care can be discussed.

If shuffling is a problem, it is important to consult with your specialist, as it can be caused by some medications.

Many elderly people with Alzheimer's may sleep more, be reluctant to move and go off their feet. They are unable to walk even with a carer at each side. They may have to be moved from armchair to wheelchair by two caregivers.

Others may be able to walk with the help of the two carers. Often I have seen residents who continue to walk with help but are on their toes all the time like a ballerina.

Sometimes changes occur over a long period of time. Sometimes there is a dramatic overnight change. Regular monitoring by specialists should be continued throughout the disease.

Aggression

Aggression may develop in a previously passive partner which the carer finds frightening and difficult to control. When a toddler has a tantrum, we cope. Distraction techniques or taking them away from the upsetting situation may work, but coping with an adult who is angry is a frightening experience for even trained psychiatric nurses.

I have known tiny ladies throw a huge tantrum scaring their alarmed, though still loving, husband. This can be a very sad part of dementia. Carers may find that they just don't know how to manage anymore.

Incontinence

The third major reason for having to give up the care of a loved one is when they become incontinent. At first it may be that they just can't get to the toilet quickly enough due to their slow walk. Then they may get into such a deep sleep that they don't wake up to go to the bathroom. Visits to friends or outings may be curtailed. When the carer has been up at 3 am changing a bed and they have to change the loved one several times a day when they are tired, life becomes very difficult.

There are many aids to help, and at first it may be possible to cope. But despite all the incontinence aids and special mattress covers mistakes happen and wet carpets, beds and furniture can be a huge problem. Winter time is not a good time for a lot of extra washing either.

The carer becomes tired and weepy and they may be elderly too.

Caregivers find that with the extra work involved and with incontinence of faeces too they may have to admit it is time for them to share the care with a residential home.

Safety

The loved one may wander off and get lost or be a danger to themselves and others in traffic. While wandering around the house they may turn on a ring on the stove or attempt to light a fire.

If a home cannot be made safe enough, then a specially designed facility or care home may be needed.

The time comes when it is not safe to leave the loved one at home. A good friend realised it was time when dashing home for lunch to check on his wife, he passed her in her car going the other way. She had found her hidden car keys. She was only 42 years old when her Alzheimer's started. He felt very sad at having to make the decision of full time care when she was only in her late forties.

Sundown Syndrome

Sundown syndrome (or sundowning) is a term used to describe why some people with Alzheimer's become more restless, agitated, or combative once the sun goes down. They may wander more, and become more distressed at this time of day and have difficulty sleeping.

Often this is a characteristic of the middle stages of Alzheimer's, and can settle down as the disease progresses. Many are mobile and wander day or night throughout their illness anyway, but if it is a new phenomenon and only occurs after dark, it may be related to sundowning.

It is thought that perhaps the part of the brain which controls the biological clock is affected. Concepts of day and night can become blurred, time is less important to them. Sundowning is another major problem which means that many caregivers cannot cope with their loved one at home.

If you have been managing any of these problems on your own at home, you are amazing. Realise that when it is time to get some more help, you mustn't feel guilty, you are to be congratulated.

WHEN IT'S TIME TO FIND A CARE HOME

Coming to terms with accepting help, or finding a care home for loved ones

One of the huge difficulties carers face is putting themselves first for a while. Having spent years caring, considering putting your loved one into a care home can make you feel like a failure. You feel guilty even thinking of putting your beloved wife, husband or parent into respite or long term care. But you must remember - you cared and did your best and that is all any of us can do. You will get feelings of "did I do enough" as everyone does. But you need to accept that 24 hours a day supervision is a blessing for your relative. It's more than you would be able to give. Some families cannot cope at all. ***Whatever happens you should be proud of the time you coped and never feel guilt.***

The quality of life for your loved one can be improved by going into long term care. They interact on a daily basis with many more people. The hard work of high dependency care is now shared by many day and night carers. Staff come on fresh to do their shifts. Activities are organised and there is a lot going on. If your loved one is still aware of their surroundings, don't be surprised if their interest levels rise for a while. If you can take your relative for a trip in the car, a picnic, or a walk, it can be a pleasure now rather than a burden.

If you are the breadwinner for your family and need to go to work every day, you may have to accept care at an earlier stage. Coping with a parent or partner with dementia is difficult and even more so if you have young children or grandchildren to cope with too.

If you are trying to manage any of the major challenges mentioned in the previous chapter, you deserve a medal and should never feel bad about getting help. These are challenges which really require professional input.

It is a difficult time. It is hard to accept that you can't cope any more, but praise yourself for what you have done. Take a lot of 'me' time now and good luck.

Finding the care needed

It can take weeks or months to get the help needed, so try to think ahead and don't leave it until you reach crisis point. An assessment may be made to define the level of care required. Then a bed in a suitable care facility needs to be found.

Try to be clear about what help you want. One friend cares for her husband at home for three months then he goes into care for one month. If you only want a few days respite it might be better to get a live-in carer at home. Nursing agencies will be able to advise you about this.

Long term beds are easier to find than respite care as homes often have no spare beds for short term care. Some homes have minimum stays of two weeks or even a month.

Questions you'll need to answer:

What about funding?

It is very important to go into the finances of care at an early stage. You will need to consult social services to see what support you are entitled to. Many homes in Australia expect families to put up bonds, as well as paying monthly fees. Fees for many homes depend on the person's means. Their pensions will be taken and a fee. Some partners have given up their homes and downsized to find the bond payment. It is a good idea to get professional advice about this early on before crisis is reached. In some countries war veterans' homes give preference to returned service men and may be more affordable.

Can friends and neighbours recommend homes?

This is useful, but it is best to visit several yourself as well. Get the whole family involved in helping to investigate the local possibilities and take someone along with you for support.

Where is the most convenient so that the whole family can visit?

What is the type of care available - is it low or high dependency?

Is there a good resident/staff ratio?

How do the residents and staff relate to one another? Is there a friendly atmosphere?

Is the home clean, well decorated and bright?

Don't be afraid to ask as many questions as you like. Make sure you talk to the matron or manager and view the rooms. Ask to see the menu and discuss any dietary requirements.

Take advice from your Doctor, social worker or the care team who have been involved.

If respite care has been place then the carer may decide to place their loved one in the same home long term. If the couple are in an over 55s complex then sometimes they can go to the nursing care section and the partner remain in his/her home on the site.

Accept that you have done a wonderful job

One of the hardest things to accept is that this is not your loved one's crisis. They are getting excellent care by you. It is your crisis because you need help. Don't be afraid to ask for this help. You have been the key pin to holding the family together for years, so be proud of yourself.

You have to look after yourself to protect your loved one. Don't forget that you are also grieving for the partner or parent who is now only a shadow of their former selves. Dementia in a family member for whatever cause is difficult for everyone concerned.

Accept all the support you can get from any source. Don't be afraid when you get low days. Visit a friend for a cuppa and shoulder to cry on. Remember you have every right to grieve. Read over again our chapter on Grieving.

Adapting to the change when your relative goes into care

Many caregivers, having been committed to full time care for many years, say they won't know what to do with themselves once they no longer have to do the caring. You may feel lost at first having had to do all the washing, dressing, feeding, shopping and household chores yourself. However, there is still lots to do. Visiting the loved one and shopping for their needs still takes up a lot of time. The total strain of the years of care you gave will take time to sink in. Normal life will return slowly. Go to an Alzheimer's family support group where you will meet lots of people feeling just as you are. It helps to talk. If there is no specialised Alzheimer's group available, go to a grief support group or a general carer's group. They will be glad to welcome you.

If you have been a caregiver, you should be so proud of what you have done. Often it is only when you have bravely made the decision that you can't cope that family and friends see what a strain it has been on you.

Visiting when your loved one is in residential care

If you find it very difficult to visit, don't feel guilty. Many people find it very hard to visit their loved ones with Alzheimer's as it can be so distressing to see them so changed. The person they loved isn't there anymore, and they may not even recognise you. This can be very upsetting.

Some members of the family always want to visit and check on their relatives and others find it very difficult. These are all normal reactions.

Don't be afraid if your loved one says that they want to go home when you visit. Remember the child who always says they don't want to go to school. Often it is to make the parent feel guilty and they enjoy it when they are there. Yes, it will all add guilt to your feelings. Yes, it is a difficult time. But talk to the staff about how they are when you're not there. Don't beat yourself up unnecessarily.

Things to organise when moving a relative into long term care

There are forms to fill in.

You need to name all their clothes with waterproof pen. Always find easy to wear clothes for them, jogging pants, T shirts with no buttons, belts or zips. Velcro fastenings on shoes or slippers are easy for staff and residents. Take home any special items you prefer to wash but ideally take in easy care materials.

The home should discuss with you any urgent needs. If the person constantly wanders or has a shuffle walk, then good shoes or well fastened slippers are required. They also tend to wear out quickly.

Never leave any valuables with your loved one. Other residents may wander and things get lost. A small amount of cash can be left with the manager if there is a mobile shop occasionally, but at this stage handling any money is probably impossible for the majority of residents.

If your relative has a wedding ring check it is not too tight or slack enough to fall off.

Organise with the home all the other care needed such as podiatry, dental care, and hairdressing.

Discuss any special dietary requirements with the manager.

Ideas to make visiting a quality time:

Try to visit when it is sunny so you can go for a walk or drive. A short walk around the garden or a longer one with them in a wheelchair is pleasant if their mobility is poor. The latter is an ideal visit when you have any children with you. Again, don't forget the sunscreen and a hat for everyone.

Visits might be difficult if your partner or parent makes little conversation. Take in old photo albums of the family so that you can look at them together and reminisce. Often the older generation like to look at any Royal family photos.

Take old postcards or cards to look at or write Easter or Christmas cards together. Let them choose and talk about the family you are sending them to.

Take a friend in to visit with you and this helps the conversation to flow.

Remember to give messages from other family members and neighbours.

Take in the local paper and read a few articles with them. The conversation may be limited now but they do still enjoy listening.

Old magazines just to look at the pictures are also useful. If they get torn it doesn't matter.

Ask them questions and give them time to reply even if this takes a little time. What did you have for lunch? Do you remember our friend Jack, he got married on Saturday? Tit bits of information to get the brain working.

It is also a good idea to take them to their room and go through their wardrobe with them. Sort out clothes that are too small or need repair, show them any new slippers or shirt you may have taken in. Talk about their favourite colour.

If you always cut your partner or parent's hair you can still do this during a visit. Talk to the staff about it. Don't use sharp ended scissors in case they turn suddenly.

Also sit and give them a manicure sometimes, put nourishing hand cream on too. They often enjoy having cream on their hands and face and also some lipstick but it's not wise to leave it with them.

If your wife or mother has a handbag, sometimes they love to sit and just take out cards, combs or small items like photos and put them back again. Just repetitive actions that seem to give comfort. An old handbag that she may have had for years will be something familiar.

Take in little gifts for them to open, it may be near Christmas, Easter, their birthday or you could take in some homemade cakes.

Friends may have sent cards or letters so it is good to read them and leave them for their room. They love to look at them often.

Visiting at activities time can show you how involved they are or not.

Take a small music player with some of the old favourite tunes on. Sometimes this gets a sing along going and the tapping of feet.

When the loved one is settled well you can take them home for lunch or tea. You and the staff will know if this is a good idea or not. Some residents want to go back to the new home as soon as they have eaten as it is their home now and they love routines.

Some homes allow pet dogs to go in. They love to stroke pets.

Like children, I have seen many residents giggling away at simple things like blowing bubbles. They do say it is our second childhood. Think of what your grandchildren enjoy doing and ideas to take in for visits will flow.

Other visitors and staff will help you with ideas too.

You will get to know other residents and families which is good, but the downside of that is, you will feel sad when the inevitable deaths occur. Just try to think positively that your visits gave them an interest too. They are at peace now and you can send condolence messages to the family.

Do limit your visits so that you have time to create a social life for yourself.

Best wishes and Happy Visiting!

Children visiting care homes

Grandchildren, nephews, nieces and neighbours' children may have been familiar with a friend or relative with Alzheimer's over the years and seen the changes in them before they were admitted. They like to know what is happening and often want to continue seeing their grandparent or friend. This is good, so plan for a positive visit. Ask the children to take in a recent photograph so it can go in the loved one's room or they could make a card for them. Younger children could do a drawing for granddad's room wall and they love making chocolate rice crispy cakes which are simple things to give.

Children are often fascinated with chair lifts up the stairs, chairs that can get residents out of them easily and other aids. Talk to the children and answer questions. Other residents love to see children around and there are other visitors and staff to talk to as well. Take in a pack of cards. Granddad might laugh at a remembered game of snap.

Children and the elderly often have a close affinity. Never be afraid of taking children in to visit.

Groups of Children visiting Care Homes

During my years running a high dependency home in a small village the headmistress of the local school and I had a mutually beneficial exchange which proved very successful for everyone involved. Once or twice a term groups of around eight pupils would come into the home and sing for the residents. The children who played instruments like recorders or piano (which we had in the home) would join in the concert. Often the residents would join in to sing a well-known song. At Christmas of course they would sing carols for us. At Easter the children would parade for us in their home-made bonnets. A resident and a staff member would chose the winners and we would give small prizes. At Halloween, they would come and scare us with their costumes and trick or treats. The workmanship that went into these costumes was wonderful. These outfits were often made at the school. Teachers would bring the children and they would parade around the home for the residents to admire their work.

Another teacher wanted her class to do a project on disability aids that were available. A small group came and were fascinated trying out the stair lift, seeing the bath hoists and bed hoists and the different walking frames. They talked to residents and were shown how to use electric wheelchairs. Several of our residents had dementia. It didn't bother the children that they followed them around to watch and listen to the class. The residents got used to the children visiting and the children got used to them.

The school hall was small so they used the large church next door for nativity plays and school concerts. Our residents were always invited and many went. Some of the children's parents were also staff so they got to know our residents well and would arrive to collect their mum after a shift and go in to say hello to everyone. Two of the children who had visited the home later became carers at the home for many years.

If their parents were working on Christmas morning many children came into the home to help with the traditional Santa Claus visit. Each resident had their own sack of presents collected from families over the previous weeks. Many relatives arrived too. From 10 am to 12 noon presents were given out by Santa. The children would help with the opening where needed and all gifts had to be marked with names. They also helped with pulling all the Christmas crackers and helping residents on with their hats. Then sherry would be served. Any residents going out with families would leave. Some husbands or wives would have arrived to have lunch with their loved one at the home. It took a lot of planning but everyone always agreed it had been fun for all concerned. It was always a few hours full of laughter. The children often said to me: "That was Brill!"

INTERVIEW WITH AN ALZHEIMER'S CAREGIVER

We are talking to a carer in Sydney, Australia who is caring 24 hours a day, 7 days a week for her husband who has Alzheimer's, and she has agreed to talk to us and answer some questions which might help you all. We will call him Joseph (not his real name).

Was it you or your husband who first noticed something was wrong and what were the first signs you noticed?

It was me. It's hard to know how far to go back because I wasn't sure whether it was just old age causing things to change. It took me a while to realise that it was more than that. And the things that were happening. He was making poor decisions that were out of character, and he had a rather unreasonable attitude to my trying to explain to him why I didn't think his decision was right.

So did he come across as frustrated or aggressive when you didn't think he was right?

He was quite aggressive.

How did you deal with that?

Sometimes the easiest way was just to give in if possible.

How long was it before you had a proper diagnosis from you noticing?

Probably 3 years.

So you were wondering for three years, what's going on?

Because Joseph had had a heart attack and had an allergic reaction to the contrast dye, they had to defibrillate him to bring him back. It had obviously caused a little bit of a problem with his confidence, so I had put it down to that for a long while. Eventually we went to the doctor who sent him for tests to a psychiatrist.

What kind of tests were done?

The normal things that a psychiatrist does like giving them memory games. For instance, giving him three words to see if he could remember them after a short span of time had passed. He did quite well with a lot of those things, especially if it was to do with drawing, circles or things as his graphic design skills gave him the better ability to do these sorts of things. He was also sent for brain scans and blood tests.

What was the diagnosis at this time?

He was diagnosed with depression at first. This was coming from the psychiatrist.

Were these tests done as an out-patient?

Yes, I also took Joseph to a specialist geriatric psychiatrist and she felt that Joseph was doing OK and we just continued seeing the psychiatrist who had diagnosed depression from the tests that had been done.

So when was Joseph actually diagnosed with Alzheimer's?

Unfortunately, it was later on when Joseph had a car accident which precipitated a hospital admission and more brain scans. Since the car accident, Joseph had had terrible anxiety and the doctors at the hospital said that there was every likelihood that the brain damage had started with the heart attack. In the brain scan there was a kind of white shadow at the front of the brain, but no sign of a stroke.

How did you both react to hearing the diagnosis?

I was very sad, but very pleased and relieved that someone had given me a real diagnosis.

Was Joseph aware?

No, he wasn't.

What happened after the diagnosis?

Joseph was more unsettled because of the trauma of being in hospital and having to go to court because of the car accident. He was aware that something was wrong and it made him very wary of me making the slightest mistake when I was driving because he felt that the police would have picked us up. But that made it very difficult for me, because he was very critical of my driving.

What did he expect the outcome of the court case to be?

I don't think he fully understood when we tried to explain to him that, yes he was responsible for having done it, but that nothing would really happen to him. We just tried to reassure him that everything would be alright. I would be looking after him and everything would be OK.

How has Joseph been since the diagnosis?

He had to give up sailing then as he wasn't allowed to drive. His friends also got to the extent that they phoned me and said they had felt that they were being a bit endangered because Joseph being the skipper steered the boat around the race course, and they felt he was making inappropriate decisions and they were quite concerned. His spacial perception doesn't seem to be very good, nor does he have a sense of time.

So he gave up his sailing and was at home with you and you got into a routine. How much care did you have to give him and how much could he do himself?

I had to remind him to do things. He was actually still showering himself, shaving himself and toileting himself. And dressing himself for a while. But then he wasn't really doing it properly. I then had to start helping him, and ask for the disabled key if we were camping.

He was walking the dog, he had lost interest in reading and his Bonsais, so his normal interests – the lot went, more or less at the same time. It wasn't as if he'd read more because he wasn't boating. He didn't really show any interest in the garden. I suppose more or less about that time was when he started having incontinence accidents too.

What are his main symptoms now?

He is social enough when anyone comes but he doesn't instigate conversations at all with anybody. He needs help dressing. I put him in the shower and I shampoo his hair and he likes to give himself a bit of a wash at the front and back and I make sure he's done his underarms. I dry him, I shave him and I dress him. He can't tell if he needs to go to the toilet, but I can run the water if I'm going to give him a shave and he'll suddenly just wee on the floor, as if he just doesn't know, or hasn't got any control. I don't wait now, it's got to the stage where there's no point asking him do you want to go to the toilet because he'll say no. So I have to say, come on let's go to the toilet every hour or two, and he invariably does.

He can feed himself but I have to cut things up for him. He used to be able to butter his toast, but he can't work that out anymore. I just put the butter and marmalade on and cut it up for him, but he can eat it himself.

What have been the hardest challenges for you as a caregiver?

Being patient. Seeing him deteriorate into this person who is only a shadow of their former self, to use that cliché. There is nothing really shared anymore, you know. Just not getting very much response from him at all, and actually to a large extent I suppose you are very tied down because they don't really want to go out.

What is your daily routine?

I'm an early riser, and Joseph seems to be quite happy to stay a bit longer. And provided he's been up to the toilet in the early hours that's fine. Well, I get myself a drink, and get the breakfast, eat my breakfast then get him up and shower, shave and dress him. He has his dentures in the solution. He's been OK so far washing them and putting them in himself. And then I get him sat down and started on his breakfast. I put a load of washing on and get the place sorted while he's eating. Quite often when he's eating I've been taking my granddaughter to work and the dog to the dog park, and then come back and he's had breakfast. Recently though, he sometimes hasn't eaten his breakfast, but has just turned all the pieces of toast butter side down. He can sometimes put his plate in the dishwasher, but other times, he can't work out how to open the door. That all takes probably an hour and half, I suppose, and sometimes slower.

What medications does he have?

He has his prescribed medications for his Alzheimer's at night which makes him drowsy. So in the morning he takes fish oil and Vitamin A and B and aspirin. He has that after his breakfast. He takes his evening tablet after his evening meal. He's got a good appetite and he sleeps well, and I'm lucky he's not wandering.

What do you do in the rest of the day?

I've usually got the washing organised and things reasonably straight before its time for a morning tea or coffee between 10 and half past. I try and get Joseph to go out in the garden in the sun, if that's what I'm going to do, but he invariably says "I'm alright here" and doesn't want to go outside. When I tell him about beautiful orchids being out, he doesn't seem at all interested.

He's always looking for a nap. He's been dozing on and off in the morning which is why I try to get him to do something but he doesn't seem to have any interest in the photo albums any more. I did try to get some of those talking books from the library, but he can't follow them. He likes the television on and sometimes there's things on the history channel that take his interest. So I just sit for five minutes and then go and do whatever I was doing, you know, wash the car, clean a few windows or do a bit of gardening, whatever. And I do the things that need doing. I just pop in and out and talk to him and just check on him. I go and do the food shopping or the post office or chemist or whatever while he's having a nap. And every now and then, I'll just say to him, right we're going to take a picnic and have a sandwich by the water and he'll come, but he's wanting to go back, as soon as he's finished his sandwich, he's done that and he'll want to go home.

After he wakes up from his nap, he'll have the television on, and if I've been busy in the morning and haven't really spent much time with him, that might be when I'll say, well, come on, I'll take the washing in and fold it and then have a game or something for a while.

Does he help you with the laundry or anything?

Well, I do say would you like to unpack the dishwasher and put away the things he knows where they go, and just leave the other things that he can't do on the bench, but he just says no. We have a push along carpet sweeper and so I think if he's been sitting for a really long time and hasn't wanted to do anything, I'll say oh, Tilly has dropped a lot of dog hair, can you push the carpet sweeper around, and he does push it round, I mean, not very well, but it's exercise for him. He sleeps well, and eats well. I'm lucky he's not wandering.

I've been trying to get him to play patience and he can still play crib if I help him, which I think is good to make him think about it. I do that whenever it fits in with whatever I'm doing. And it not at a specific time. So he's not looking for me to do it at a specific time. Just random.

What time does he have afternoon tea or supper?

He has got no taste for cups of tea at all and hasn't had a cup of tea for weeks. He just has water. He has orange juice at breakfast. He might have a slice of cake or a biscuit at afternoon tea time. Then we have our meal at between six and half past roughly depending on whether I've been down to pick up our granddaughter.

After dinner and before bed, I don't play games with him, he's too tired, and invariably I'm too tired too. I'm still usually clearing the kitchen or whatever.

He goes to group one day a week from half past ten to half past two. I take him. He could be picked up on the bus but you could be standing there for half an hour or more for it to come, and when he first started we had a lot of wet weather, so I got into the habit of taking him. And then I do the dog at the dog park, you know, in the one trip and that seems to suit alright. But they bring him home on the little bus.

Could he have more days if you wanted to?

He could, but he doesn't want to go and I'm not forcing the issue.

Do you have friends round or take him to family or friends?

We haven't actually been out to do that very much of late. I have a very good friend and I like to go and see her and spend time with her without Joseph and a lot of friends I feel don't know how to handle somebody with a problem like Joseph's, so we haven't really been included. Most of our menfolk still work, and so it's not quite the same and he's happier at home so in some ways it's easier to have people to our place, but then that doesn't happen all that often.

What advice do you have for other caregivers about the daily tasks involved?

Don't fuss about what you can't do. You can only do what you can do. I suppose to a large extent I try to be fairly optimistic about these things and I know there are lots of people who are caregivers who are in a more difficult situation than me. I am fortunate that I'm giving care to somebody who is fairly quiet, doesn't wander and sleeps well, although at times it can be hard, not as difficult as the stories I've heard from other people. Just take one day at a time and sort of work out what suits the both of you.

What support have you had from agencies?

I was given information about groups of people who give home support. I was told that they would come and sit with my husband if he didn't want to go out. Or they said they would take him out in the car or driving or something like that, and Joseph was very averse to wanting to do this, and was quite concerned about having strangers in the house and not wanting to go anywhere with strangers and so I didn't pursue that avenue. I haven't felt the need to have cleaners in. And so that particular care service I haven't availed myself of. There is another service, which is a Commonwealth service and they will do an emergency care for a few hours, but I don't think it's a sleep over type of arrangement but there is a telephone number that I was given that I can use for assistance.

When it became obvious that Joseph was becoming more dependent on me I was advised to get in touch with a group of people called ACAT which is Aged Care Assessment Team and one of their people came to interview us in our home and asked dozens and dozens of questions, of Joseph mainly, and with a bit of assistance from me.

It took about 10 days to two weeks and we got a report back and Joseph was deemed to be high care. This is something that is non-revocable and stays available for Joseph from that day on. I was not informed at the time that I if I wanted respite care I had to organise it myself, but in due course I did get that sorted out and approached various aged care places to see if they did do respite, and have been fortunate enough to have a break, which I think is well worth doing, as difficult as it is to put your loved one in care. But it was the best thing for us both to have had that break.

Why didn't you allow the carers into your home?

I did feel at the time that I was coping OK and while I was coping I thought I would continue to do so. They did say they couldn't give you a specific time as they didn't know how long they'd be involved with other clients. And as you can understand, they explained to me that everybody would like to be the first in the morning. And that's not always possible, and I didn't fancy two o'clock in the afternoon or something. So while I was managing I thought I'd carry on.

How do you feel you are coping?

I think I'm coping OK. There are some days when I get a bit down and perhaps a wee bit short tempered, but it doesn't last long because I know it's not his fault. You've got a job to do, so you get on and do it.

I think I'm fortunate that Joseph is quiet and doesn't wander. I know there are a lot of people worse off than me. I'm also lucky that I am reasonably fit and that I have had the stamina to keep going.

Do you get help from family and friends?

I get support verbally from family and friends. I get people who phone me to see how things are going, and if there was ever a need I know they would come at a drop of a hat to help me, and that's all very reassuring to know that they are there if I need them.

Do you ever think you can't cope anymore?

No, not yet. I do wonder sometimes how long it's going to go on for.

How did you come to terms with deciding to get some respite care?

I could feel myself getting tired and getting emotionally upset about things and realised that in the best interests of us both I needed to have a change or a rest.

How did you go about organising it?

Phoning around to find a place and then going and looking at it and finding out what sort of services they offered and what the place was like. I had heard about a place that it was good, and when I went there my first impression that it was nice and bright and airy and friendly staff, and I felt that it would be suitable. I was very fortunate that a vacancy came up in a reasonably short time and I was able to avail myself of it. I felt it was necessary that it was near home, so that it made it easier for family and friends to call in and they could reassure Joseph that I would be back.

How did Joseph handle the respite care? Does he remember it?

Yes, he does remember it. He wasn't very impressed with the food, he said, but he couldn't tell me what was wrong with it! He didn't feel that he needed a holiday, so it was difficult to explain to him that he needed go and give me a chance to catch my breath. He hasn't ever mentioned it unless he has been asked a specific question.

What other things do you do to look after yourself?

I play bridge sometimes which is good.

I have friends who invite me to go out for nice lunches occasionally. I did have a nice holiday when Joseph went into respite which was very good and recharged the batteries. I took my daughter away for three nights and then came back home and went away with a friend. I didn't go and visit my husband during that time. Part of it was that I didn't want to have to go in and then leave him, and also that I wanted him to be more settled so he wouldn't have me coming and going and him wanting to come back home. Our sons went in pretty well every day and some friends called in to see him.

Have you booked any more respite care?

I have, I was advised to try and take a break every 3 months, which I think is probably a very beneficial thing to do and so to make sure that I don't miss out on getting a place for Joseph I have booked one in less than 3 months, and then another one three months after that.

Do you think about what the future holds? Or just take things a day at a time?

Basically just take things a day at a time. If I say I'm not planning things ahead that's not true as I have actually decided that respite is necessary. It'll all depend on Joseph I suppose and how he goes. I don't know how long I can keep going, and I don't know whether I keep going out of pride or because I want to prove that I can cope.

Any further comments or advice for other caregivers?

Don't feel guilty about things that you feel you should be doing but haven't been able to do. That's something I have to practice myself a lot more, but it is how I feel. You try to do the right thing and get them doing things.

I used to get Joseph to go out and water his Bonsai trees when the weather had been hot, and it was something he used to like doing. The only problem was that when he had finished doing it, I'd have to completely change him and his socks and shoes, as he had lost the ability to do it without getting himself completed soaked too! So what do you do? It's your choice!

Also try to keep a sense of humour. Sometimes you just need to laugh at the silly things that happen. I asked Joseph to turn the light on as I was popping out to pick up my granddaughter for 10 minutes and it was getting dark. When I came back, he got up and turned the light off. Oh, he said, when I touch that it gets dark!

RESOURCES

These websites contain all the resources you will need. They contain the most up-to-date telephone helplines, and most have online forums where you can get support.

USA

http://www.alz.org/

http://www.alzheimers.org

http://www.caregiversunited.com/

http://www.nia.nih.gov/alzheimers/publication/caring-person-alzheimers-disease

UK

http://www.alzheimers.org.uk/

www.chill4us.com

www.alzheimersresearchuk.org

Australia

http://www.fightdementia.org.au

Worldwide

http://www.alzheimersreadingroom.com/

http://www.griefandsympathy.com

ACKNOWLEDGEMENTS

I would like to thank my daughter Lesley Postle who is the editor of this book, without whom it would never have come to fruition. We are also deeply indebted to the following people for their warm support, encouragement and helpful suggestions: Andrew Postle, Andre Poublon, Wendy Chen and Edna Fairley. A special thank you to our interviewee for her honest answers to questions and her dedication to facing the new challenges of each day. Over the years, I found it a great privilege to work with many wonderful people with dementia and their families, and I would like to thank all of them for everything they taught me.

DISCLAIMER

This book is intended as a guide to provide general advice and support to caregivers. It should not be regarded as a substitute for proper medical advice and support. If in doubt, please consult your doctor, specialist consultant or social workers.

Made in the USA
Monee, IL
24 June 2021